TOP 50 QUESTIONS

Skeletons

SEYMOUR SIMON

SCHOLASTIC INC.

New York Toronto London Auckland Sydney
Mexico City New Delhi Hong Kong Buenos Aires

To Joyce and our grands: Chloe, Jeremy, Joel, and Benjamin, from Granpa with love

Acknowledgments

Special thanks to Nancy Sabato for her excellent design and to Alison Kolani for her skillful copyediting. The author is grateful to David Reuther for his editorial and design suggestions, as well as his enthusiasm for this project. Also, many thanks to Gina Shaw, Suzanne Nelson, and Carla Siegel at Scholastic Inc., for their generous help and support.

Photo Credits

Front cover: © Neil Guegan/zefa/Corbis; back cover photo and page 16 (knee): © SPL/Photo Researchers, Inc.; page 1: © John Watney/Photo Researchers, Inc.; page 3: © Digital Vision/Getty Images; page 4 (foot): © Stockdisk/PictureQuest; page 4 (scale): © Royalty-Free/Getty Images; page 6: © PictureQuest; pages 4 (hand), 7 (vertebrae), and 9 (pelvis): © Anatomical Travelogue/Photo Researchers, Inc.; page 5 (left): © Philip Dowell/Dorling Kindersley/Getty Images; page 5 (right): © Michael Abbey/Photo Researchers, Inc.; page 7 (ear bones): © Dave Roberts/Photo Researchers, Inc.; pages 8, 10 (arm), 11 and 14 (jaw): © Ralph Hutchings/Visuals Unlimited; page 9 (femur): © TRBfoto/Getty Images; page 10 (thumb): © AbleStock/PictureQuest; page 12 (top): © Andrew Syred/Photo Researchers, Inc.; page 12 (bottom): © Lester V. Bergman/Corbis; page 13: © Bill Longcore/Photo Researchers, Inc.; page 14 (tooth insert): © Steve Gschmeissner/Photo Researchers, Inc.; pages 15 and 26: © Biophoto Associates/Photo Researchers, Inc.; page 16 (hip joint): © Dr. Don W. Fawcett/Visuals Unlimited; page 17 (top): © Dr. Robert Calentine/Visuals Unlimited/Getty Images; page 17 (ear): © Christine Pedrazzini/Photo Researchers, Inc.; page 18: © Salisbury District Hospital/Photo Researchers, Inc.; page 19: © Chris Bjornberg/Photo Researchers, Inc.; page 20: © Zephyr/Photo Researchers, Inc.; page 21: © Steve Allen/Getty Images; page 22: © P. Motta/Photo Researchers, Inc.; page 23: © Voisin/Photo Researchers, Inc.; page 24: Davies & Starr/Getty Images; page 25: © Richard T. Nowitz/Corbis; page 27: © Joe McDonald/Corbis; page 28: © Ron Kimball/Photex/zefa/Corbis; page 29 (top): © Ted Spiegel/Corbis; page 29 (bottom): © Jules Frazier/Getty Images; page 30: © Louie Psihoyos/Science Faction; page 31: © Martin Dohrn/Photo Researchers, Inc.

ISBN 0-439-79598-2

12 11 10 9 8 7 6 5 4 3 2   6 7 8 9 10 11/0

Printed in the U.S.A.
First printing, September 2006
Book design by Nancy Sabato

chapter 1

HUMAN SKELETONS

① Why do you need a skeleton?

Your skeleton helps you to stand, walk, run, jump, and move. Your skeleton also protects important organs such as your brain, heart, and lungs. Without a skeleton, your body would collapse.

2 How much does your skeleton weigh?

Your skeleton makes up less than one fifth of your total weight. So if you weigh 100 pounds, your skeleton weighs less than 20 pounds.

3 What are bones?

The bones in your body don't look like the dry white sticks you see in a museum. They are living parts of your body that grow and change as you age. Living bones have blood vessels and nerves and are about one-third water.

4 How many bones are there in a human body?

Adults have 206 bones in their bodies.

5 Do children have more bones than adults?

When children are born, they have about 300 bones in their bodies. But as they grow older, some of those bones join together, or fuse.

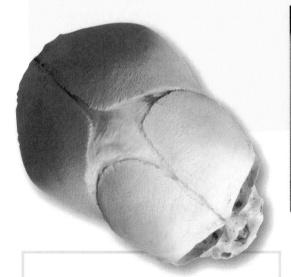

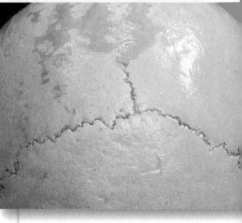

You can see that there are fewer bones in this adult skull. The bones have grown and are closer together.

A baby's skull has more bones than an adult skull because the bones are not yet fused together. The bones are also farther apart.

PARTS OF THE SKELETON

⑥ What is the skull?

The skull is a hard bony case that supports and protects your brain, eyes, and inner ears. The *cranium* is the part of the skull that encloses the brain. It is made up of eight bones that fit together like the pieces in a jigsaw puzzle. Fourteen bones form the protective framework for your eyes, nose, cheeks, and jaws.

⑦ What are the smallest bones in the body?

hammer

anvil

stirrup

The smallest bones in your body are three tiny bones in each ear. They are named the hammer, the anvil, and the stirrup because of their shapes. These bones pass sound vibrations to your inner ear so that you can hear. The stirrup is only about one eighth of an inch long, smaller than a grain of rice.

⑧ What is a spine?

The spine, or backbone, is a column of small bones called *vertebrae* that run down the middle of a body from the skull to the pelvis.

⑨ What are vertebrae?

Vertebrae are hard, hollow bones that protect the nerves in the spinal cord.
Your spinal cord carries messages between your brain and the rest of your body.

vertebrae

spinal cord

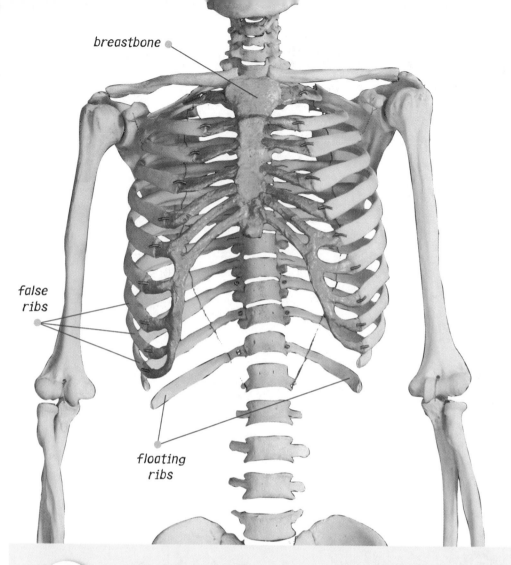

breastbone

false
ribs

floating
ribs

⑩ Why do we need ribs?

Ribs are flexible but tough bones that protect your heart,
lungs, and other important body organs. The top seven
pairs of ribs are joined to the spinal column in back and
to the breastbone in front. Your muscles move the ribs in
and out when you breathe.

11 What are false and floating ribs?

The eighth, ninth, and tenth pairs of ribs are joined at the front to the ribs above but not to the breastbone. They are sometimes called false ribs. The bottom two pairs of ribs are not joined to anything at the front. They are sometimes called floating ribs.

12 What is the pelvis?

Your pelvis is the bony cradle that joins your spine to your legs. It is about halfway down your body. You can feel part of your pelvis when you touch your hipbone. The pelvis supports and protects the organs of your lower body such as your intestines.

13 What is the longest bone in your body?

The longest bone is the *femur*, or thighbone. It connects the top of your hip to your knee. Leg bones are longer and thicker than arm bones because they carry the weight of your body as you stand, walk, and run.

14 Which bones make up your arms?

The *humerus* is the large bone that connects your shoulder joint to your elbow. Your forearm connects to your hand at the wrist. The two bones in your forearm are the *radius* and the *ulna*.

humerus

15 How many bones are in your hands?

You have 27 bones in each hand, one more than you have in each foot. There are 8 wrist bones and 19 finger bones. Your thumb has three bones and your other fingers each have four bones. Your hands are both strong and delicate. You can use them to pick up a large rock or a tiny grain of sand.

radius

ulna

What is your "funny bone"?

The "funny bone" is not really a bone. It is a sensitive spot in your elbow where a nerve runs over the end of the ulna. If you accidentally hit your funny bone, it feels as if a jolt of electricity has passed through your arm.

funny bone

Your thumb is a pretty amazing digit. If you throw a ball or pick up a coin, your thumb is facing all your other fingers. That's why we call your thumb opposable. An opposable thumb allows people to do all kinds of things with their hands that can't be done otherwise. Try picking up this book or holding a few sheets of paper together without using your thumb and you'll see how difficult it is.

HOW BONES WORK

17 What are bones made of?

Bones come in different sizes and shapes, but most have a hard, solid outside called *hard bone*. Hard bone is made of living bone cells that form rings around tiny canals through which arteries and veins pass.

18 What's inside a bone?

Many bones are hollow, making them light but strong. The spongy tissue inside a bone is called *soft bone*, or *marrow*. Marrow contains special cells called *stem cells*.

19 Why do we need bone marrow?

The hollow centers of many bones are filled with soft marrow. Marrow makes red and white blood cells and a material called *platelets*. Red blood cells carry oxygen to all the cells in your body. White blood cells help fight disease and germs. Platelets help the blood to clot after an injury.

20 Are there other ways bones help us?

Bones store the *minerals* you get from food. The minerals are what make bones hard. When minerals are needed by other parts of the body, they are released from the bones into the blood. Teeth, nails, and muscles need calcium and other minerals. Minerals also help regulate *blood pressure* and *heart rate*.

21 Are teeth bones?

Teeth are not really bones because they are made of *enamel* rather than hard and soft bone. Babies' first teeth appear when they are six or seven months old. Most kids have 20 baby teeth by the time they are three years old. By age five or six, children start losing their baby teeth. These teeth are replaced by 32 permanent teeth.

Beneath the surface enamel of a tooth is a bone–like material called dentine, shown in green.

muscle

22 What are muscles?

Bones don't move by themselves. Whenever you walk, breathe, or turn the pages of this book, muscles move your body. When muscles contract, or get shorter, they move the bones to which they are attached. When muscles relax, they get longer and they don't pull on the bone to which they're attached. Muscles usually come in pairs, so while one muscle pulls a bone one way, the other muscle relaxes.

tendon

23 What are tendons?

Muscles are attached to bones by ropey tissues called *tendons*. Tendons help pull a bone each time a muscle contracts. You can see some of your tendons along the sides of your neck and behind your knees.

kneecap

24 What are joints?

The point where two bones connect to each other is called a *joint*. In some places, such as your skull, the joints are locked together. But most joints allow the bones to move easily against each other.

25 Are there different kinds of joints?

Ball-and-socket joints in your hip and shoulder let your bones move in any direction. Hinge joints in your knees and fingers allow back-and-forth movements but not side-to-side movements. Other kinds of joints are called saddle, pivot, and sliding joints.

pelvis

cartilage

femur

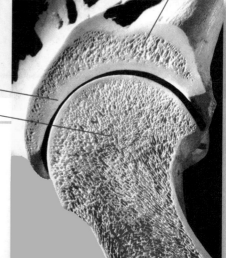

The hip joint allows movement between the pelvis and the femur. The joint is rimmed with cartilage and lubricated by a fluid. The bones are kept in place by ligaments and moved by muscles.

26 What does cartilage do?

Cartilage is a white, rubbery tissue that cushions bones where they connect to each other at your joints. Cartilage allows bones to move easily across one another.

27 Where can you see cartilage in your body?

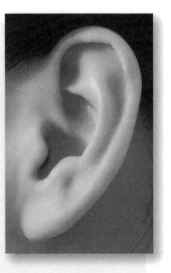

The outside, flexible parts of your nose and ears are made of cartilage. Your *larynx*, or voice box, is also made of cartilage.

BROKEN BONES

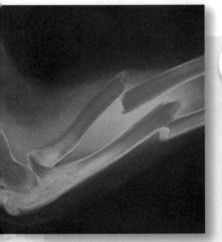

28 What happens when a bone breaks?

Even healthy, strong bones can break or *fracture* as a result of a fall or accident. Simple fractures break the hard exterior bone. Compound fractures also pierce the skin and damage the surrounding blood vessels and nerves.

29 How can we see bones inside the body?

X-ray machines can show bones inside a body. An X-ray machine shoots *electrons* through the body. X-rays pass right through flesh but bones stop them. Newer machines called CAT scans use computers to give us a clearer picture of bones.

30 How do doctors help bones to heal?

Doctors reset broken bone ends so that they can grow back together and recover their full strength. Hard casts made of plaster of paris or soft casts made of plastic are often used to keep a bone in place so it can heal properly. In some cases metal pins are inserted into broken bones to keep them together.

31 What is an artificial knee?

When a knee is badly damaged by injury or disease, doctors can replace the damaged bone and cartilage with an artificial knee made of metal and plastic.

32 Can doctors replace a hip?

If a person's hip joint is damaged, these bones can be replaced with an artificial hip made of plastic and metal. An artificial joint is called a *prosthesis*.

33 Are there other artificial joints?

Shoulder and wrist joints can also be replaced. The goal of any joint replacement is to stop pain and allow a person to move more easily.

(34) What is osteoporosis?

Osteoporosis is a disease that causes people to gradually lose some of the minerals in their bones. These bones become less strong and are more easily broken. Osteoporosis happens in some people as they grow older.

35 How can we strengthen our bones?

You can help build strong bones by eating healthy foods that contain the minerals and vitamins you need, especially calcium and vitamin D. Getting regular exercise also strengthens your bones and muscles.

36 What are artificial bones?

Scientists have developed steel and plastic materials that can be used to replace bones or parts of bones that are lost through injury or disease. Artificial bones can help people who have had bad bone breaks.

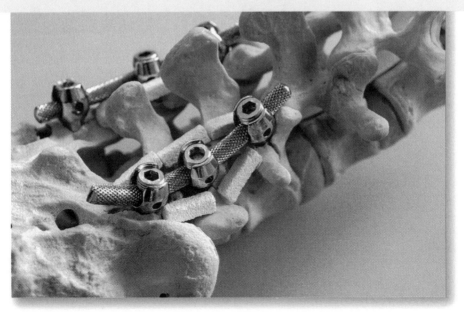

chapter 5
ANIMAL SKELETONS

37 Are animal skeletons different from human skeletons?

Animals with spines, such as humans and other mammals, birds, reptiles, amphibians, and fish, are called *vertebrates*. Animals that do not have spines, such as insects, spiders, and shellfish, are called *invertebrates*.

38 Can a skeleton be outside an animal's body?

Insects, spiders, lobsters, crabs, shrimp, scorpions, and many other animals have outside skeletons that cover their entire bodies like a suit of armor. In order to grow, these invertebrates have to shed their old skeletons. Then a soft, new skeleton hardens in its place. Clams, mussels, and oysters live inside a shell, which is another kind of outside skeleton. These shells do not have to be shed as the animal grows. Instead, the shells just grow larger and larger.

39 What is the smallest animal bone?

The ear bones of a hummingbird and the rib bones of a guppy are the smallest animal bones.

40 What animal has the largest bone?

The jaw of a blue whale is the longest animal bone, over 20 feet in length. That's about as long as a midsized automobile.

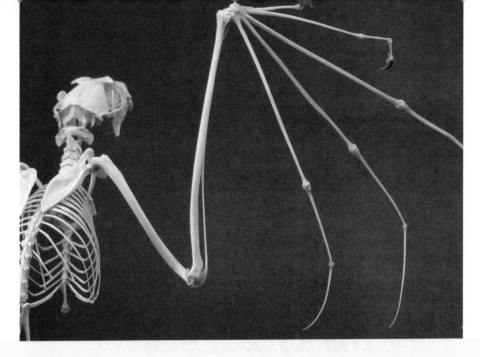

41 Do birds and bats have arms and fingers?

Yes, inside bird and bat wings are arm and finger bones much like those of land animals. The main flying feathers are attached to the arm bone and two long fingers.

42 How does a fish's skeleton help it swim?

Like all vertebrates, fish have a bony skull and a backbone. But fish also have special bones called *fin rays*. These bones keep the fins stiff and spread out so that they can push against the water and move the fish forward.

43 Which has more neck bones: a sparrow or a giraffe?

A sparrow has 14 neck bones while a giraffe has only 7. A sparrow's neck is more flexible so that it can turn its head easily. A giraffe needs large neck bones to hold its head steady.

44 How can a snake swallow food larger than its head?

Snakes can open their mouths very wide because their upper and lower jaws are loosely connected by a double-hinged joint. This allows a snake to swallow prey much larger than its head.

(45) Are an elephant's tusks made of bone?

No, elephant tusks are very long front teeth. A large male elephant can grow tusks 7 feet long, taller than most people. A long elephant tusk weighs over 100 pounds. Imagine having teeth that heavy in your mouth!

46 Are horses' hooves bone?

Horses walk, trot, and gallop on the tips of their toe bones. A horse's foot has one long toe bone covered by a horny hoof that is like your fingernail, only much tougher.

47 Which animal bones grow the fastest?

Antlers, which are made of bone, grow the fastest. Deer, elk, and moose can grow a full set of antlers in just five months.

48 What are animals' horns made of?

The horns on cattle, sheep, and many other mammals are made of a bony core surrounded by a material called *keratin* that is like your fingernails.

(49) What have fossils taught us about bones?

Fossils are the remains of long-dead animals or plants that have turned to stone over millions of years. Fossils let us learn about the skeletons of animals that no longer exist, such as the dinosaurs. Dinosaurs had gigantic bones, some of which were 9 feet long.

50 What's most important about your bones and skeleton?

Your skeleton makes the strong framework your body needs to walk, run, eat, and breathe. And the insides of bones make the blood cells your body needs. Without your skeleton, you wouldn't be YOU.

INDEX